The Individualist Doctrine

Laszlo Miklos Zsidai

The Individualist Doctrine, by Laszlo Zsidai

First Edition

ISBN: 0999547801

ISBN-13: 978-0-9995478-0-9

To my wife, Tammy, who has supported me through all of our adventures, good or bad. To my sons, Laszlo and Landon, whom I love dearly and wish only a better and freer world for in the future. To all the people who desire and fight for freedom.

Table of Contents

1: Journey of Discovery

Tom Hilton, *Traffic*. Flickr.

As you sit in your car, wait for a train, board a plane, or ride a subway to go to your place of employment, do you feel your life slowly being taken from you, like you are not in control?

You know that you control your body, actions, places you go, conversations you have, and decisions; however, for some reason you don't feel in control of your life or of where your life is going. The news, television shows, magazines, social media, friends, community leaders, and politicians tell you why and how you should feel about the events around you, what is right or wrong, and who is popular and who is not. The reasons they give are because of race, religion, economic standing, nationality, or the place where you were raised. They claim that if you just follow their guidance and directions, donate your money, and vote for them, then your lot in life will improve, and you will feel better about yourself and your community. Simultaneously, these tolerant, righteous, know-it-all people claim that if you differ from their position, then you are an outcast, uneducated, a bigot, or maybe even disturbed and should be shunned and ridiculed. Against your better judgment and instincts, you listen, follow their guidance, and do your best to take on their ideas and positions—but to no avail. Your family isn't improving, your troubles still remain, you don't feel any happier, and you and your family are harder off now than before. It doesn't seem right; you know this but don't want to admit it. Some are so mired in the guidance, more aptly called propaganda, that they are consciously oblivious; but they too can feel deep down that something is off, if not plain wrong. In either case, you can't seem to understand why it is wrong or feels wrong or isn't getting you where they promise. This uncertain feeling is the beginning of your **AWAKENING,** and realization of your true surroundings; as hazy as it may seem at first, like newborns opening their eyes for the first time, you start to see where you actually stand.

After some thought and through experiences, you realize that control and direction of your life are being taken little by little from you. Simple tasks you did when a child now require some city permit, government approval, license, or fee to pay, or are downright illegal. Be it cutting down a tree on your property, setting up a lemonade stand, starting a business, practicing your faith, or raising your family, there are now rules and laws. There are some rules that make sense and many you can rationalize why they may be needed, but frankly some are just ridiculous, against common sense, or outdated.

As time goes on, you seem to realize that these seemingly ridiculous rules, tasks, and hurdles you must jump over are implemented so that control and direction can be taken from you, little by little, in such a manner that they hope you won't notice. And many people don't notice, many don't care or ignore it, some put up with it and push through; but **YOU HAVE NOTICED,** and so have others. Now that you have noticed, you try to discuss or ask questions about it but may not know how to articulate your feelings or thoughts on why it is wrong or feels wrong. Some will try to articulate it and end up being called names, mocked, or worse—socially declared prejudiced or paranoid. But to your surprise, through continued discussions of your concerns, you find others and others find you who share similar feelings and experiences. As you speak with these people, your thoughts and feelings clarify and crystallize. So you seek out more people, information, continued education, reading, discussion, and opportunities to listen to liberty-oriented content on the radio, television, or the Internet. You further frame, clarify, and crystallize your thoughts and moral compass on these feelings and issues. In fact, all these positive interactions bolster your confidence that **YOU** are in fact on to something.

At this stage, you will find your first major hurdle. With this newfound confidence, you talk to your family and friends to try to open their eyes too, only to be told that you are being silly, reading too much into things, not fun or boring. They will try to convince you that you are wasting your time and should pursue other activities instead of politics and these boring issues. That it doesn't matter. This hurdle should be realized as a success: those around you are hearing your opinions and are starting to question their comfortable, cozy, blindly guided beliefs and positions and would rather try to silence you then to questions the supposed fundamentals of their beliefs or positions that they hold so dearly, but for unknown reasons. This does not mean that you force your opinions onto others or be rude; rather, know that you are starting to make cracks in the wall that so many people have built around their lives and minds, as prescribed to them, to remain comfortable, ignorant, and controlled.

However, what exactly you have discovered still escapes you, so you keep learning, searching, working, and producing. You keep at it; the thought keeps gnawing at your mind, but you tire of not being able to determine what exactly you have discovered until one day the inability to express your feelings lifts, and it becomes very clear, it is simply—

FREEDOM!

Unknown photographer, *August Landmesser Almanya 1936.* Wikimedia Commons.

2: Arriving at Realization

You say it to yourself again—**FREEDOM?** It sounds silly, something out of a movie, or a conspiracy theory so subtle. You realize that you are slowly and covertly losing your freedom, but you know the signs and fear the tyrannical, collectivist, serfdom that awaits. Shortly after this realization, you become aware of just how encompassing this issue is, and the thought of resisting is daunting. But what frightens you even more is becoming a slave, a serf, to some faceless masters and that same fate befalling your family, friends, and especially your children or grandchildren.

Your political, social, economic, and religious **BELIEFS ARE UNDER ATTACK**. The common-sense fabric of life, liberty, and the pursuit of happiness is being unraveled behind flashy events. These flashy, in-your-face issues and events don't really mean much to your freedom or your life but try to capture your attention so that you don't see what you're losing and your freedom is being taken.

If the loss is unnoticed, who will resist? Maybe that is the key and what they are hoping for! But you have noticed and have the desire to **STAND UP AND FIGHT** against this tyranny for yourself, your family, friends, community, state, and country. It is time for you to awake from your slumber and **RISE**. Rise and begin breaking the chains that hold us down—

RISE AND RESIST!

3: Rise and Resist

You now know that you must **RISE AND RESIST**, but you are not alone; there are many others. A legion of men and women who are also tired of the encroaching shackles of slavery, who are tired of feeling directionless and powerless, who strongly desire to bring back what is almost lost; and to regain **FREEDOM**, the **SPIRIT OF EXCEPTIONALISM**, to regain and place the power back in the hands of the original and only minority—the **INDIVIDUAL**!

Austin Kirk, *Wind-Torn American Flag in High Key.* Week #11 in "52 of 2014." *Flickr.*

As you have heard, witnessed, or even experienced firsthand, your freedom is unraveling. Your individual freedom is under attack, your family is under attack, and your property rights are under attack through silly rules, regulations, red tape, and groups advocating taking what you have worked hard to earn.

Economic freedom is being hampered and perverted. Starting a business, operating a business, innovating, patenting, hiring, and firing are all being dictated by massive layers of regulations and bureaucracy. In many cases it is worsened because political insiders have decided who the winners and losers will be. There are many examples: government bailouts of banks and automotive companies, corporate welfare, phony programs set up to support businesses that otherwise couldn't support themselves, or social programs with good intentions funded through the economic activities of others who never have the program's lack of success questioned or suggest the program be reformed or even ended. All of these are supported through forced charity on the backs of tax payers with no real input.

Unknown photographer, *Polish priests and civilians at the Old Market, Bydgoszcz, 1939.* Wikimedia Commons.

Religious freedom is slowly being stripped away through round about laws, judicial decisions, or political edicts by numerous politicos who care not for your beliefs or faith. They argue that division of state and religion is required; however, somehow that also means schools, all public places, and even the national anthem should be scrubbed of any religious words or innuendoes, ignoring the deep-rooted purpose of why those words were there in the first place. In reality, they are trying to prevent parents and communities from raising their own children with morals and values that differ from the government and central controllers. They do not want you to raise children who may be future free-thinking individuals, or more aptly—future opposition.

Social and political freedoms are being eroded at an alarming rate. Identifying for one or another political party gets you labeled as one thing or another, be it prejudiced or a kook. Educating others about history and truths may even land you the title of denier or extremist; they will try to draw parallels between you and real extremists, terrorists, or mass murders to ruin your reputation and smear you. Those same people who advocate for equality, free speech, and tolerance will then use government, police, and regulations to tie your hands, seize your property and money, silence you, and possibly even put you in jail to prevent and stifle all dissent

Urbán Tamás, Romania, Transylvania, Timisoara. ID 31879. Fortepan.

against the current narrative they wish to foist on the masses. Simultaneously, these same people lie, collude, and do terrible, heinous things without question or consequence, yet alone facing justice.

These supposed intellectual elites will use the same tired, boring, and pathetic reasons why we should forego our freedoms for the "greater good," "the public benefit," "national security," "for the state," or "to help those less fortunate or needy." The path they advocate has been tried for centuries and has failed, unlike individualism, the Industrial Revolution, and the fantastic standard of life that freedom and capitalism have brought. Numerous examples can be provided of the true end that the ideas they push will cause, like current Venezuela, or past obvious examples like the USSR, Nazi Germany, and tyrants such as Mao, Castro, Che, and Stalin. Furthermore, the horrendous outcomes to the public that those tyrants brought with them—oppression, starvation, squalor, millions of deaths, and war—are not mentioned or even considered.

In essence what they are really preaching is simply, "Give your power, your vote, your independence, and freedom to me, who is smarter than you, to solve society's problems and make everything better", and at the same time also saying, "Keep calm while I place these shackles on your hands and feet and steal your wealth and freedom."

We must resist the bait they are trying to lure us with or else find ourselves and our families caught in their tyrannical hook. We must **RISE AND RESIST** these temptations and hardships. We must move onto the—

OFFENSIVE!

the red flag on 25 February 1848. Wikimedia Commons.

4: Move on to the Offensive

Those who seek to control us have a great deal of breadth but not necessarily depth in their control. They predominately achieve their control through the passivity of the large public masses who are currently sleepwalking through life, confused, or busy with cheap entertainment. Through your journey of resistance, you will continually be hampered by these people; they will be an annoyance and a barrier, but they are not all our enemy. They are future recruits to our legion, when they too have achieved awakening and the fog of confusion has lifted. Our real enemies are those above them, the ones who push and direct the tyrannical agenda, which can fall under many disguises and terms—such

Archives New Zealand, *Will You Fight Now or Wait for This Recruitment?* Flickr.

as socialism, fascism, progressive, nationalism, modern liberalism, equality, and fair share, to name a few. The ones who don't listen but only preach to and punish those who don't unquestionably follow their commands and directives—they are the true enemy. They are the mini-tyrants.

They have filled our communities, counties, states, and federal governments, including numerous agencies, with their believers. The passive sleeping masses allow them to pursue their oppressive agendas. It is through these layers of agencies, bureaucrats, laws, and regulations that we will **FIGHT** through and **WIN!**

We are producers and workers; we know what hard work is and how to overcome obstacles and barriers. However, this fight and push through needs to be approached with great care, as traps will be laid. We must seek out the weaker agencies to find positions in them and while there, learn and take notes, slow down the progress, and convert or abolish those agencies first. We must work our way up to

Production Drive Committee, *All Out for Victory*. NARA, 534920.

harder and harder agencies and win those over. As we move from small victories to medium victories to large victories, we will absorb and increase the ranks of our legion through those that awake. Those who join the cause may show us other agencies or weaknesses that we can and will exploit. We will continue until we **WIN!**

Production Drive Committee, *Production Is the Thing That Will Get That Swing; Let's Step It Up*. NARA, 534601.

Those who knowingly implement or aid in the implementation of rules, laws, or regulations to lessen freedom and do not care to change, even after being shown their folly and the many lies, need to be stripped of their power and removed from their positions peacefully. These victories and the reasons for freedom need to be broadcast to the passive public masses so that our enemies hear it as a battle cry, and our family and friends hear it as a—

CALL TO ARMS!

Norman Lindsay, *The Trumpet Calls.*

5: Call to Arms

Those reading this have probably realized already that this is exactly that—a **CALL TO ARMS!**

Fellow freedom loving friends—take pause—evaluate your surroundings, and see what and who you are working for, toiling for, and paying. Do they help or hurt our cause? Do they help or hurt you, your family, community, and freedom? Of course, this may be hard to answer—or worse, the answer is they are hurting the cause of freedom. Do they deserve your effort and productivity? If not, you are aiding those who wish to shackle you. So again, I urge you to assess yourself, your family, and your community to begin aligning as many aspects of your life and actions in such a manner that they aid the cause of freedom. Associate with people and businesses that aid you and freedom, and voluntarily support those that also support the cause of freedom. Conduct business, start businesses, and educate and learn from these likeminded individuals to aid each other's productivity and prosperity, while simultaneously depriving our enemies of your productivity, money, effort, and innovations.

As you change your life, family, and community through voluntarily aiding likeminded people who support the cause of freedom, your communities will improve, your feelings and resolve will improve, and emotionally you will feel empowered. Note that this does not happen overnight; for some it may be quickly realized, while for others it may take years. Eventually, others will look to this and so too desire it; through education, they will join our legions and aid our cause. Both of these will deprive our enemies of resources, money, and people, causing them to figuratively starve. As they starve, their tactics will be increasingly desperate. It is for these reasons we need to be careful; we must continue to resist, but wisely, against their tactics. When they are sufficiently deprived of resources and productivity, this is when our legions will advance on their strongholds.

We will take over city councils, legislatures, the Senate, bureaucracies, and judicial seats through elections and appointments. We will take over and further the cause of freedom in those agencies, through reforms or abolishment of those agencies. Through increased education and freedom, more people will awaken and join our legion. If you look carefully, you will notice that his has already begun.

Jean-Adolphe Beaucé, *Siège de Puebla, 29 Mars 1863.*

As our ranks swell, the use of force against us will become an ever-higher possibility. The use of counterforce must be thoroughly and carefully considered and resisted, especially when we respond to these violent tactics perpetrated on us by our enemies. However, it should be clear that we shall defend ourselves as appropriate. We will voluntarily band together and aid each other in this struggle. We will implement **FREEDOM** and—

THE INDIVIDUALIST DOCTRINE!

6: What Is Freedom?

This brings us to the question, what is **FREEDOM AND THE INDIVIDUALIST DOCTRINE?** What exactly is our cause, and how do we achieve this at home and abroad? Our doctrine is simple, and to achieve that for ourselves, our family, our communities, and our country, the following ideas and policies shall be advocated and instilled in all people who strive for **FREEDOM AND INDIVIDUALISM**:

1) Support our freedom loving allies through voluntary exchange, productivity, money, and votes, thusly starving our enemies.
2) Implement or strengthen freedom of speech rights.
3) Implement or strengthen private property rights.
4) Instill or strengthen the right for people to bear arms.
5) Shrink the roles and responsibilities of the governments at all levels to only those activities absolutely necessary as outlined in the Constitution

or governing and founding documents (military, international trade, justice, etc.).

6) Implement capitalism and free trade internationally, especially with those countries and nations that reciprocate.
7) Demand competition in all industries and services, and end government monopolies (education, transit, healthcare, etc.) through private competitive means.
8) Eliminate the death tax, the inheritance tax, and other forms of taxes and fees between generations.
9) Simplify the tax code through a flat tax on all income for all people and businesses, and repeal and reduce laws and regulations curtailing freedom for individuals and businesses.
10) Decentralize credit from a singular government bank to multiple competing private banks.

Some of the above seem self-evident as to why, while others may not.

SUPPORTING FREEDOM LOVING ALLIES will help strengthen our allies and bolster their finances, thus providing an additional cushion of independence from the government or those who wish to control us. Simultaneously, this will deprive our enemies of gaining money and buying power. This may mean person to person, business to business, country to country, or any combination.

FREE SPEECH, PRIVATE PROPERTY, AND THE RIGHT TO BEARS ARMS are the foundation of what made America so different and successful from other nations plagued with tyrannical monarchs or governments throughout history. The simple fact that one can speak out, own property, and have the means to personally defend it, be it from foes within or outside the nation, makes it harder for anyone else to control such an individual. This power dynamic has seldom existed in other nations, where usually the members of the populace were unarmed and vulnerable, more like helpless sheep: unable to defend themselves and afraid to speak out.

George Caleb Bingham, *Stump Speaking.*

SHRINKING THE ROLES AND RESPONSIBILITIES OF GOVERNMENTS to only those absolutely necessary prevents the government for attaining a dictatorial position over the people they are to represent. If the government is able to direct all aspects of your life through regulations, that essentially becomes the same as having a slave owner who states what you can or can't eat, whether you are or aren't allowed to cut a tree in your backyard, or forces you to buy a product you don't want, as some examples.

IMPLEMENTING CAPITALISM AND FREE TRADE INTERNATIONALLY allows many economic advantages to all players, such as comparative advantage. Additionally, countries can adapt their industries as technology changes and they harness innovations and economies of scale. All these benefits are to the betterment of the customer and ultimately people.

ALL INDUSTRIES AND SERVICES SHOULD BE COMPETITIVE AND WITHOUT MONOPOLIES throughout society to discourage cronyism, corruption, poor service, and high costs. Rather, the customer should be cherished and fought over, not ignored and used.

THE DEATH TAX, THE INHERITANCE TAX, and the like only hamper the people on the middle and lower economic spectrum, as the wealthy have means to avoid or maneuver around these laws and regulations while losing a minimal amount of wealth and thus retaining their wealth advantage over those who would challenge their monetary position in society. This would allow families to save and aid their future kin and relatives to help advance their families in society.

SIMPLIFICATION OF THE TAX CODE AND A GENERAL REDUCTION OF LAWS AND REGULATIONS to the bare minimum are essential in reducing the encroachment of government and bureaucracies in our society. As the laws increase, the number of people required to run them increases, as do the monies collected from taxpayers to fund these agencies. Added bureaucracies also increase the potential for cronyism and corruption. With tax codes simplified to a flat tax, the masses do not need to fear government revenue agencies, file hordes of silly paperwork, or hire armies of lawyers and accountants in an attempt to save their hard-earned cash. This also eliminates the continued need for lobbyists and special-interest groups from influencing the government to make an already complicated tax code more complicated but beneficial to one particular group.

Lastly, **DECENTRALIZE CREDIT** from a singular government bank. This is to prevent one group of people making important decisions that could cripple entire nations' economies or suggest certain monetary or financial directions that benefit a few at the expense of the many, under the guise of helping a nation in recession or avoiding a depression. Too often, as history has shown us, these small groups of people fail to make the correct decisions, causing the masses to suffer and ultimately bail out the corrupt wealthy. Having multiple banks allows different decisions to be made by each and thus allows solutions that work for many, not a solution that works only for a few.

Howard Chandler Christy, *Scene at the Signing of the Constitution of the United States.*

The above doctrines need not be carried out in numerical order for success; however, the first four ideas and policies should be implemented as quickly as possible to aid in implementing the others faster and achieving **FREEDOM** sooner.

This **CALL TO ARMS** seems daunting, but it is **NOT**, as the desire for life, liberty, and the pursuit of happiness is inherent in all people. Some people will wake slower from their slumber than others and some not at all. As **FREEDOM** is regained and the spirit of independence and liberty grows, it will fill more and more of our people to strengthen their resolve, and they too will wake others from their slumber. As more people join, our cause will advance faster and faster. Therefore, my friends and allies, **RISE!**

RISE from your foggy slumber foisted upon you, and fight for your freedom and happiness. Let us once again bring true life, liberty, and the pursuit of happiness to ourselves, our families, our communities, and our great nation. Let your desire for freedom become the fire we use to melt the shackles that others try to put on us to control and enslave us.

RISE!

REGAIN YOUR FREEDOM!

REGAIN YOUR INDIVIDUALISM!

Emanuel Leutze, *Washington Crossing the Delaware,* 1851. MMA-NYC.

Notes

About the Author

Laszlo Miklos Zsidai is a Hungarian-born Canadian immigrant whose family successfully escaped communism. He was raised in a good home, with typical immigrant parents pushing academics, and he moved a great deal. He graduated from the University of Toronto with a BASc in materials engineering and from McMaster University with an MEng in nuclear engineering. He is currently pursuing his MBA at the University of North Carolina. He has worked over the last twelve years and across multiple industries, most notably about ten years in the nuclear industry in diverse roles, and internationally for about six years. He currently works to promote and implement proton therapy, a less-invasive cancer treatment solution, across the globe. He is a husband to a great woman and a father to two awesome boys. As a result of diminishing global poverty and suffering, increased economic freedoms, and overall betterment of mankind, Laszlo strongly believes in capitalism, freedom, and individualism.

Made in the USA
Monee, IL
09 November 2026

67972897R00029